PUTTING SOUL

INTO BUSINESS

How the Benefit Corporation is Transforming
American Business For Good

MARY ANNE HARMER

TOM HERING

Book Cover Design: Tessa Milhollin (tessamilhollin.com)
Interior Formatting: Tracy Yates (proebookformatting.com)

ISBN: 978-0-692-93934-5

Dedicated to our greatest source of inspiration:
Christopher, Nicole,
Cameron & Ross

*We are extremely grateful for
Ruth Miles' ardent support of small businesses
and in-depth knowledge of Benefit Companies.*

CONTENTS

INTRODUCTION

"The times they are a changin'."
— Bob Dylan

We are living in a time of fast, incredible change. Everywhere you look the old way of doing things is rapidly going the way of the dinosaur. We don't have to tell you that is particularly true in the business world.

Yet of all the changes we've seen, we believe one stands out above all others. Because it has the power to do what has rarely been done before: put soul into business.

Enter the Benefit Corporation.

In our minds, we feel the Benefit Corporation is the catalyst for a better business, a better community and a better world. Yes, we know these are lofty claims but read the simple, yet powerful definition:

> *In addition to profit, the Benefic Corporation includes positive impact on society, workers, the community and the environment as its legally defined goals.*

We aren't so sure the State of Maryland knew it was starting a national movement in 2010 when it became the first state to introduce this business game-changer for companies. But seven years later, you'll find more than 33 states offering the Benefit Corporation and 6 states with pending legislation. It's safe to say that it is a movement all states will soon be behind as well as companies who want to make a positive statement to their stakeholders.

Why it makes sense to American business is no mystery. Every day, we learn more and more about the accelerating challenges in social justice and the environment all across the country. Global warming and equity issues seem to dominate news channels week after week. When combined with the changing demographics of the American workforce and our communities, we can say this without a doubt: *The status quo no longer represents the social, environmental and multicultural values of our country.*

Consumers are advocating for these changes using their pocketbooks. A 2015 research study by Nielsen reports nearly 66% of global online consumers across 60 countries said they are willing to pay more for products and services by companies that are committed to positive social and environmental impact. These are convincing numbers all by themselves. But when you consider that the report also stated that the willingness to pay more is consistent across all income brackets, you have data that simply can't be ignored.

In another 2015 report, this one conducted by Cone Communications which focused on Millennials in the U.S., research found that 70% are willing to pay more for products and services of companies with corporate social responsibility programs (CSR). 70%! The study also suggests that female Millennials appear to be the most loyal supporters of those companies with a willingness to:

- Buy a product with a social and/or
  environmental benefit, given the opportunity
  (90% versus 83% adult average)

- Tell their friends and family about a company's
  Corporate Social Responsibility efforts (86%
  versus the 72% adult average); and,

- Be more loyal to a company that supports a
  social or environmental issue (91% versus 87%
  adult average)

All of which gives the two of us hope.

It should do the same for you. Because we believe the
Benefit Corporation is going to be a strong catalyst for
growth by the companies who adopt and practice such
contemporary thinking in the months and years ahead.

It is our intent in this book to not only show why you
should embrace this entity for your own business, but
how to do it. Along the way you'll read about
companies both large and small and learn about their
decisions to become a Benefit Corporation. We believe

you will find the transcripts of their interviews with us inspiring. It certainly was the case for us as we talked with these forward-thinking yet humble leaders.

After finishing the book, it is our hope you jump in and become part of this fast-growing movement and embracing what a short while ago seemed almost impossible: *putting soul into business.*

Mary Anne Harmer

Tom Hering

Chapter 1
WHY THE TRIPLE BOTTOM LINE

*"It creates a buzz when you have a value
proposition that is more than just about creating a
product for sale and profit. It is the only way to
grow our business, and every year since we started,
our sales have increased."*

— Hussein Al'Baity, Founder & CEO, The Printory

We're betting that many of you have heard of the
"Triple Bottom Line." Whether you became first aware
of it from a news site, business event or in a client
conversation, it's an idea that is right for your company
and right for the times. As you're about to learn, the
Triple Bottom Line lies at the very heart of the Benefit
Corporation.

6

The phrase was coined more than two decades ago by the founder of a British consultancy. His name is John Elkington. Back in 1994, he argued that companies should be preparing for not one but three different bottom lines.

The first is the measure of profit. The second, people, is the measure of how socially responsible a business is. And the third, planet, according to Elkington, measures how environmentally responsible the business is. His belief, and one in which we share, was that only a company that produced a Triple Bottom Line takes into account the full cost of conducting business.

Why we're telling you this is simple: Benefit Corporations embrace the Triple Bottom Line also known as the "3 P's." We believe it is the sacred mantra for the times. And we aren't alone. Portland, Oregon's largest family-owned and operated brewery, Hopworks Urban Brewery (HUB) is an example and sources local ingredients to enrich the local economy and reduce their carbon footprint. "Pursuing the Triple Bottom Line is a reflection of a modern business reality," says Christian Ettinger, Brewmaster and Owner of HUB.

"Everyone else will soon be playing catch up."

We definitely agree with his comments as employees, prospects, customers, community members and all other stakeholders will continue to hold businesses accountable going forward. And as you might have guessed, their measuring sticks will always be framed around the 3 P's.

Now let's look a little more closely at the reasons for these three essential components.

People:

Throughout the 20th century, businesses appeared homogenized. That is, for the most part, they looked, acted and thought alike. But as time passed, huge changes have occurred in our workforce and businesses. The people inside today's companies resemble nothing like those employees just a few short decades ago.

The most obvious difference: You will find more gender and ethnic diversity across most industries. What might not be so obvious is that diversity is a major contributing factor for business growth and success. In a recent study conducted by *McKinsey Group*, the researchers found 10 positive economic correlations resulted when diversity is present in a company. These include: increased innovation, a greater pool of capable talent, more satisfied customers and yes, an increase in profits.

What does this mean to businesses today? We find 4 obvious conclusions:

- Employees no longer solely reflect a singular Western European value and belief system.

- Employees no longer reflect the style and thinking of traditional Baby Boomers (or their parents).

- Employees no longer reflect the "traditional" American values of "Mom, God and apple pie."

- Leaders are no longer just white, straight and male.

As business continues to evolve, we must invest in people with a new understanding, sensitivity and empathy. After all, we are bringing together different cultures, abilities, generations and lifestyles.

Bottom line: we are absolutely convinced this diversity of people, thought and behavior is not only good for business. It's good for the world.

Planet:

You cannot say it's theory anymore. Global warming is a reality. (As we write this, an iceberg the size of Delaware broke off the Antarctica ice shelf!) Just consider these compelling statistics revealed and shared in numerous respected research studies:

- *34%*: the amount of carbon dioxide in the atmosphere that has risen since the 17th century

- *1,000,000 + species*: the number already facing extinction due to global warming

- *7 - 23 inches*: the estimates of sea levels rising by the end of the 21st Century

- *1*: the current rank of the U.S. as a global warming polluter

- *400,000*: the number of Arctic Sea square miles already melted due to global warming

- *2030*: the year the number of glaciers in Glacier National Park will be zero

- *9*: the number of consecutive years among the 25 hottest annual temperature averages in history

Future generations depend on contemporary businesses practicing sustainability. Corporate policies must be put into place designed to save our natural resources. "Businesses that speak about but don't have a way to quantify their sustainability claims are nothing more than their marketing departments at work," adds HUB's Ettinger when asked about the environment. We need to move beyond the hell-bent focus of today's profits at the sacrifice of tomorrow's planet.

If saving the planet isn't enough of a reason to be environmentally friendly, consider this. "Green" is cool with new and emerging consumer demographics such as Millennials and Generation Z (those born between 1997 - 2012). As the earlier data showed, these generations are very selective about who they do business with many basing their choice after investigating a company's approach to social and environmental issues. Much of this holds true for Baby Boomers who marched in the original Earth Day parades supporting environmental protection.

Remember: These enlightened consumers are your prospects and customers. And they are being more selective as they make purchases, often using sustainability as the single most important factor in determining their purchasing decisions.

In the future, your customers will be won or lost based on your company's sustainability practices. No matter what size the company, every business can put environmental policies and practices into place. Together, if we all do our share, we will leave a healthy planet for the generations to come.

Profit:

The reason we saved our discussion about profit for
the last is simple. We believe that if you follow the first
two P's (People & Planet), you will reap the profit. And
yes, profit is still a positive and motivating factor
driving American business.

For starters, profit inspires companies to take risks, to
innovate, to change and excel. What's more, American
businesses need profit to not only cover their
operational costs, but also for research and
development, for investments in new green
technologies and facilities, for training, for employees
to share in company successes, for philanthropy and
more.

We also believe the world grows and stays healthy
when it is aligned with a simple profit motive, but at
the same time allows for giving back to the community.
With no apologies to Gorden Gekko, prototagonist
from the 1980s film *Wall Street*, greed is NOT good.

Which begs the question: how much profit is too much
profit? We believe in a sharing economy where all can

support their families and enjoy the fruits of their labor without extravagance or excessive materialism. This is the thinking behind People, Planet and Profit. This is the practice sparking the movement of Benefit Corporations.

Chapter 2
MILLENNIALS: THE MOST CAUSE-DRIVEN GENERATION IN HISTORY

"Millennials hear about our B Corp status and it does attract talent out of school. People love B Corps and that's a reason why they come to us."

— Sarah Joannides, Director of Social Responsibility, New Seasons Market

Millennials were born into the technology age. They lived through the horror of 9/11, the dot-com meltdown and the rapid rise of global warming. They've also witnessed greed and corruption on Wall Street on a grand scale.

Today's Millennials, those born between 1981 and 1997, wear their values on their sleeves. They strongly believe in and support social causes. They become rabid fans of businesses linked to those causes, namely environmental, equity and social justice issues. If you don't find these characteristics powerful, think again. Millennials represent $2.45 trillion in spending power.

Of this group, 60% are more likely to engage with companies that discuss social causes. But the research says there is a catch: if companies want to be effective, they need to be thoughtful and genuine about the causes they support. Or as we say, "walk their talk."

In Cone Communications 2016 Millennial Employee Engagement Study, the researchers report that by 2020 more than 50% of U.S. workforce will be part of that generation. "Millennials are coming to work seeking greater purpose and involvement in their company's corporate social responsibility (CSR) commitments," write the Cone study authors. "Whatever their job description may say, they want to know they are making a difference and they expect their employers to show them the way."

Here are some other relevant statistics regarding Millennials from the Cone research work:

- *64%* of Millennials consider a company's social and environmental commitments when deciding where to work

- *64%* won't take a job if a company doesn't have strong corporate social responsibility (CSR) values

- *75%* would choose to work for a responsible company, even for less money (versus 55% U.S. average)

- *83%* would be more loyal to a company that helps them contribute to social and environmental issues (versus 70% U.S. average)

- *88%* say their job is more fulfilling when they are provided opportunities to make a positive impact on social and environmental issues

We were absolutely blown away by this data. It gives the two of us tremendous hope as we have Millennial children of our own. In our work, we tell prospective clients without hesitation that if they want to attract the "best and the brightest" of the Millennial generation, they need to have principles and practices in a place that resonate with this generation. The framework behind the Benefit Corporation and John Elkington's 3 P's of People, Planet and Profit has a strong appeal to Millennial cause-driven values.

The leaders we interviewed for our book said without hesitation that their status as a Benefit Corporation or B Corps is a strong magnet for bringing in exceptional people to their businesses. And as you just discovered, Millennials are the future of the workforce. In interviewing Millennials currently employed, the Cone study further revealed:

- *Less than 33%* are engaged at work

- *44%* expect to leave their job within two years

- *85%* want opportunities to help employers reach Corporate Social Responsibility (CSR) goals

- *88%* want employers to share details of CSR commitments

- *89%* want to provide feedback, ideas and solutions to improve CSR efforts

- *89%* want hands-on activities around environmental responsibility in the workplace

We see the Benefit Corporation and all it represents as a classic "right time, right place" opportunity for businesses who understand the power of this data. In our minds, it could not be more compelling. By becoming a company who practices the 3 P's, you will not only become a magnet for exceptional talent as an employer, but you will also be aligned with what the marketplace today and into the future is searching for in products and services.

As Augusto Carneiro, CEO of Nossa Familia Coffee in Portland, Oregon, whose entire workforce is made up of Millennials, says, "It's helped enhance our culture. We were hiring people that already cared about the B Corp designation. But it reminded us of how important that is to prospective employees. It's been a hiring tool as prospects tell us Nossa Familia aligns with their personal values."

Chapter 3
BOOMERS: EMBRACING THE SPIRIT OF BENEFIT CORPORATIONS

"I think that we as a society are increasingly looking to create meaning in our lives. One of the ways that happens is that people make purchasing decisions based on alignment with core values."

— Jon Blumenauer, CEO, The Joinery

It was the Age of Aquarius. Baby Boomers threw off their parents' shackles. Then they broke the rules. They raised their voices, listened to a new revolution in music and embraced the communal living lifestyle sparked by the "Summer of Love" and San Francisco's Haight Ashbury district.

Yes, it was a time of rebellion and experimentation. Boomers fired up the "Peace Movement," with its iconic logo, lived through the Civil Rights movement, saw Vietnam War protests and helped launch the Women's Movement.

Boomers were always challenging and questioning the status quo as no other generation before. Nothing seemed sacred. Yet, as this generation entered their 20s and 30s, many became a part of the mainstream American workforce chasing success, seeking more money, more material goods, more power and prestige.

As of 2015, Baby Boomers number 82.3 million in the U.S. Many of them remember the cultural values learned in the sixties which continue to simmer and tickle their conscience today. Your authors are a part of this group and along with our peers believe the work is never done until we truly have healthy communities and equity for all.

Some of us have experience as industry professionals and know we have more to contribute. Rather than retire, we start our own businesses, volunteer for cause-driven organizations or assume active roles on nonprofit boards focusing on the "greater good." We embrace recycling, march for community causes and, like Millennials, use our pocketbooks to demonstrate our belief in social justice, equity and environmental issues by doing business with companies that practice the 3 P's.

A great example of such a company is Prichard Communications, a strategic communications firm providing communications, marketing and public relations to changemakers across the U.S. including the Robert Wood Johnson Foundation. "We put a lot more energy and effort into supporting our employees and using more sustainable practices since becoming a B Corp," says Mac Prichard, Founder and President of the Portland, Oregon company. "We now offer our staff annual bus passes, we compost regularly, and our financials are much more transparent."

Boomers' purchasing power is a force to reckon with. A 2015 article in Huffington Post based on data gathered by AARP (American Association of Retired People) characterizes the generation with these stats:

- Rank as *#1* consumer-age demographic in the United States

- Own *63%* of U.S. financial assets

- Spends *$3.2* trillion annually

- Account for *half* of all consumer expenditures

- Living *longer* and *better* than ever before, feeling more youthful than their predecessors and remaining engaged, active, and fulfilled

Boomers are also committed to saving the planet for their grandchildren. But this should come as no surprise. After all, Boomers participated in the first national environmental movement in 1970 known as Earth Day. Some took a step farther and became part of the activism that helped pass the Clean Air and Clean Water Acts in 1970 and 1972.

Today, given the reality of global warming, many of our fellow Boomers have renewed their activism. They demand that companies address the pollutants and waste previously accepted. Some research shows that

Baby Boomers are even more environmentally engaged -- think Al Gore -- than any other generation. In 2015, a survey of Baby Boomers revealed:

- *66%* were worried about exposure to poor air and water quality

- *92%* preferred less toxic construction and maintenance materials

- *97%* desired high-energy efficient heating and cooling systems for their home

- *89%* felt strongly that, "it is in our self interest to improve our energy independence"

- *85 %* were interested in a home with a smaller carbon footprint and less operating costs

This is why we believe Benefit Corporations appeal to our generation. These businesses have at their core strong environmental practices and include in their operating principles initiatives to preserve the planet. Given a choice, we are convinced many Boomers will choose to do business with a Benefit Corporation over a more traditional business model.

No doubt there is more to a business than the traditional bottom line. Companies can make a profit and still give back. "B Corps represent progressive, influential companies committed to being leaders in changing communities for the better," adds Mac Prichard."We are kindred spirits."

Chapter 4
DIVERSITY: DRIVING THE "BENEFIT" MOVEMENT

"B Corps represent small but influential companies committed to being leaders in changing communities for the better. We are kindred spirits in support of equity."

— Mac Prichard, Founder & President, Prichard Communications

A few years back, major newspapers wrote headlines predicting that in one generation "minorities would be the new majority." Those articles made us think about cultural competency and the importance of respecting the diverse values of a changing nation.

But the change happened much quicker than forecast.

Today across the country, even in our own predominantly white state of Oregon, more than 50% of kindergartners entered school as non-Caucasian in 2016. Just take a look around you the next time you're at the store, in a school or inside an office building. Chances are good you see a palette of faces reflecting diversity unlike anything older generations have seen and certainly different from the immigrants of our parents' and grandparents' generations.

In King County, which covers most of the Seattle area, more than 50 different ethnic groups coexist. As the analogy goes, it is no longer a melting pot, but more accurately a robust salad with distinct tastes that aren't blended, but retain their inherent flavor creating a broad experience of different flavors.

This means within our companies, there will be new ways of thinking. There will be new ways of problem-solving and communicating. The dominant western European approach to business with linear, analytic thinking will be augmented by circular and intuitive approaches to management that reflect a non-Anglo style. "I've been inspired by TOMS Shoes and other international cause-driven organizations," says Hussein Al'Baity, CEO & Founder of The Printory in Beaverton, Oregon. "What I have observed is that these businesses are compassionate, kind, authentic, inclusive in hiring, risk-takers and brave! These traits foster innovation and success."

Moving forward, the new world is not going to revolve around the individual leader who pushes forward as the "Warrior Champion" claiming victory over competitors or colleagues. Rather, the values that reflect the diversity in the workplace will spark a community approach with shared accountability. This will require commitment to the collective "WE" in leadership. Cedric Herring, a professor of sociology at the University of Maryland, states "A diverse workforce yields superior outcomes over homogeneity because progress and innovation depends less on lone thinkers with high intelligence than on diverse groups working together and capitalizing on their individuality."

With a more diverse workforce, we believe the time to be humble is important to counter our traditional communication styles and attitudes of the need to be right. We need to be open and develop a sense of humility to learn from other cultures. This suggests "alpha work heroes" will no longer flourish shouting their importance as an individual. Contemporary "work heroes" will be those who are most collaborative and embrace a communal approach.

We believe inclusivity is very much aligned with the philosophy of Benefit Corporations. Companies practicing this business model often are more successful than other similar companies. And we aren't the only ones saying it. Research from a 2015 McKinsey study of diversity supports it:

- **15%**, the number by which gender-diverse companies are more likely to outperform their peers

- **35%**, the number by which ethnically diverse companies are more likely to outperform their peers

Catalyst, the leading nonprofit organization with a mission to accelerate progress for women, finds that companies with women on the board are higher performers. Deloitte research shows that inclusive teams outperform their peers by 80% in team-based assessments. And finally, in the 2015 Deloitte research study "High Impact Talent Management," which evaluated more than 128 workforce practices in 450 global companies, the researchers conclude, "Companies that embrace diversity and inclusion in all aspects of their business statistically outperform their peers."

As you learned in chapter 1, the 3 P's starts with People, or as we say, the engine that fuels everything else. Benefit Corporations embrace diversity of thought among their employees. And there is more data to highlight the importance of such thinking. According to Deloitte's research, the two most important areas that correlate with the highest performing companies are about inclusion and diversity. These companies are:

- *2.9* times more likely to identify and build leaders

- *1.8* times more likely to be change-ready

- *1.7* times more likely to be innovation leaders

"Over the past year, we have a number of interview candidates come to us because we are a B Corp," says Jon Blumenauer, CEO of The Joinery in Portland, Oregon. "They wanted to work for a company that shares their values. This has helped us bring some great new people on board who are providing energy and leadership to improve further."

Isn't sparking innovation and growing leadership the coveted cornerstones of every forward-thinking business?

Chapter 5
GETTING TO THE HEART (AND SOUL) OF BENEFIT CORPORATIONS

"We started out as a nonprofit, but we wanted to have a greater and deeper impact and grow as a company. When Oregon passed the legislation allowing for incorporating as a Benefit Company, it was the right time to launch Sudara as a business."

— Shannon Keith, CEO & Founder, Sudara Inc.

So far, we've talked about how the three largest U.S. consumer demographic groups have expectations of companies they choose to do business with. How organizations believing in and practicing the 3 P's can look forward to a growing and loyal customer base in the years and decades ahead.

Now it's time to cut to the chase and learn what makes a Benefit Corporation different and how does your business become one, plus a reality check if you choose to follow that path.

First, you need to know that this business structure is more than just a nice philosophy. Benefit Corporations are established legal entities in 33 states with pending legislation in 6 more states as of the third quarter of 2017. These states give companies the option to register as a Benefit Corporation or in our state of Oregon and Maryland, as a Benefit Company which also allows for incorporation as a Limited Liability Company (LLC) Given this compelling data with more than two-thirds of the country now offering such an option, we believe it's only a matter of time before all 50 states will have enacted legislation for this progressive business structure.

By definition, Benefit Corporations are *businesses that consider their impact on society and the environment in addition to making profits.* This legal designation protects companies that want to strive for more than just returning money to shareholders. If a profit is generated, a Benefit Corporation is not required to return all profit to these shareholders. Benefit Corporation designation allows your company to integrate your values and mission to serve others into business practices. In other words, it doesn't have to be all about the bottom line.

Here's what our State of Oregon's website says (Other states have similar language):

> An Oregon Benefit Company is a type of corporation or limited liability company that wants to consider its impact on society and the environment in the business decision-making process, in addition to earning a profit. Benefit Companies differ from traditional corporations and LLCs with regard to their purpose, accountability and transparency. The purpose is to create a general public benefit, which is defined as "a material positive impact on society and the environment, taken as a whole, from the business and operations of the company."

"We pride ourselves on being ethical and socially responsible," says Kristopher Lofgren, owner of Bamboo Sushi in Portland, Oregon, an Oregon Benefit Company. "Making a profit is a good thing, but being able to also do the right thing is more important." This 'doing the right thing' is a shared feeling among other businesses who have adopted this legal structure. "Our customers tells us that they want to bring their business to a company that isn't driven solely by profit, rather that profit is the result of doing business the right way with staff that feels energized, supported, and believes in giving back," adds Hussein Al'Baity, CEO & Founder The Printory based in Beaverton, Oregon. "I'm always surprised when they say they really respect me when all I'm doing is sharing my bounty with others."

Initially, a commitment to environmental and social causes may seem costly. But we assert that the benefits of positive branding and relevance to new customers, particularly with Millennials, will outweigh any additional costs up front. "I can't see a scenario where this structure would not be appropriate," says Shannon Keith, CEO & Founder of Bend-based Sudara, Inc.

"We all want to build healthy communities."

The Requirements of being a Benefit Corporation

Many businesses are afraid that there is a lengthy process and a lot of paperwork in becoming a Benefit Corporation. But it is easier than you think. The most important requirement is really simple:

> *Believe in the underlying premise of*
> *Benefit Corporations and be prepared to*
> *act like one!*

There are, of course, other requirements that companies need to be aware of once they decide to incorporate as a Benefit Corporation. Check with your Secretary of State's office but in general the five common steps you need to follow are to:

1. *Include a statement* in your Articles of Incorporation or Articles of Organization that states the corporation, or LLC in Oregon or Maryland, is a Benefit Corporation (Company) subject to your state's laws.

2. *Adopt a third party standard.* (Some states ask for this only as a best practice but don't require it.) A number of companies use as a third party standard, B Lab's rigorous B Corps standard (more later), which is a highly-regarded and prestigious standard, but that is not for everyone. You will find other entities to evaluate your business for adherence to the standards associated with Benefit Corporations with potentially less process and at a lower certification fee. These include:

- The Global Reporting Initiative

- GreenSeal

- Underwriters Laboratories

- ISO 2600

- Green America

- BenefitCorp.net is another resource that provides a list of other third party standards providers.

3. *Prepare a simple annual benefit report* identifying how your business supports People, Planet, Profit. The specific content requirements for benefit reports may differ slightly from state-to-state. The benefit report supports the transparency requirement of Benefit Corporation legislation. This report details:

> *i.* The activities undertaken by your business that provide a specific public benefit. This can include pro bono work for nonprofits, sustainability measures the company follows, and human resources practices.

> *ii.* How well the company met or exceeded the third party standards.

4. *Distribute the annual report* to company owners and/or members.

5. *Post the annual report* on the company's website or make it available publicly. (Requirements many differ from state to state.)

We can tell you first-hand that even as a 2-person firm, an LLC in the state of Oregon, these requirements are very doable. Many other smaller companies like ours have done it successfully. And if you are in a state that recognizes Benefit Corporations, but does not include LLCs, there is a fairly straight forward process to modify your structure, reorganizing as a corporation, which will then enable your company to file as a Benefit Corporation. It is important to check with the Secretary of State's office within your state to understand the steps to restructure your LLC to become a Benefit Corporation.

The most challenging requirement seems to be the production and distribution of an annual benefit report. (You can learn our simple process to do it here: www.hcollaborative.com/benefit-corporations)

The third party evaluation of your company regarding adoption to principles of Benefit Corporations includes reviewing your operating principles tied to the 3 P's. If you are sincere about what you are doing, this review should be simply a way of sharing your practices and values, aligned with the vision of Benefit Corporations.

Although each of these third party entities have a slightly different approach to the evaluation, the process generally involves answering a number a questions and perhaps a phone interview.

Generally, the questions focus on the business' adoption of initiatives or practices in the following areas:

- Community Engagement

- Sustainability

- Diversity/Equity

- Purpose/Cause

- Stewardship

- Leadership Traits, including transparency, authenticity

Often the third party evaluator will ask for specific examples or documents that demonstrate these values. These could be a mission statement or accounting of community activities. For companies just launching, it is important to share the intent or future plans that show your vision toward furthering the 3 P's.

The annual "Benefit Report" is also pretty straight forward. All you need to do is create a 1 - 4 page listing of activities and initiatives that have taken place over the prior year illustrating the "spirit" of Benefit Corporations. It doesn't have to be fancy. It just needs to be an accounting of what the business did, from policies to actions that demonstrate fulfillment of requirements.

Some states do not exercise regulatory oversight of Benefit Reports. However, several attorneys "in the know," predict increased scrutiny and more rigor with potential auditing of these requirements as the Benefit Corporation movement becomes actualized in all 50 states.

Finally, about the reality check we mentioned at the beginning of this chapter. We've heard more than once about prospective customers viewing company websites who claim social and environmental practices, but in actuality it was only in theory and words. Unfortunately, they were not doing what they claimed.

And these customer or employee prospects not only didn't do business with the company but often made sure that the company's false sustainability claims were exposed on review sites such as Better Business Bureau and Yelp.com. The lesson is to be sincere and authentic in your efforts.

Which is why we will repeat this previous sentence:

> *Believe in the underlying premise of Benefit Corporations and be prepared to act like one!*

In other words, "walk your talk!"

Chapter 6
HOW BENEFIT CORPORATIONS DIFFER FROM B CORPS

"It's about being values-driven and having a commitment to the community, practicing authenticity, transparency with your employees and setting an example for corporate peers."

— Jaime Athos, CEO, Tofurky

We get asked many questions about Benefit Corporations. The most common one is, "What is the difference between a Benefit Corporation and a B Corp?" The answer is that B Corps are businesses meeting the standards set forth by B Lab, a nonprofit organization whose tagline is "measure what matters."

They may or may not be a Benefit Corporation. B Lab evaluates companies around a number of metrics. "You can't improve things if you can't measure," says Amy Prosenjak, President & COO of A To Z Wineworks. "It's as applicable to business life as it is to personal life."

So, put simply, B Corps are businesses that have chosen to pursue a rigorous, comprehensive evaluation to meet the highest standards associated with the values of Benefit Corporations. To earn B Corp status, a company must accumulate adequate points and meet certain metrics through a lengthy and robust survey administered by B Lab every other year.

Needless to say, it takes time, effort and dollars to go through the robust B Lab evaluation. But once you get designated as a B Corp for fulfilling high standards, you can announce to the world your business is part of this elite and growing group of businesses around the world.

We find the B Corp standards high but often worth striving for as a business grows and becomes more sophisticated. In fact, we set it as a goal for our own firm. It is a strong differentiator and brings with it high marketing value and cache. The problem is that many people think being a Benefit Corporation equals being a B Corp. This is not true.

Remember being a Benefit Corporation is not only about the values of People, Planet and Profit. It is also about the legal protection allowing a company to consider the interests of all stakeholders, not just shareholders. We find many Benefit Corporations practicing the 3 P's and fulfilling the requirements, yet, never go through the B Lab evaluation process for certification. But they are still dedicated to the principles. In fact, a number of startups find it difficult to initiate the B Lab evaluation process because many of the questions ask for at least 12 months of data and trends which new companies just don't have.

We believe the B Corp evaluation is best suited for more established, often larger companies as many questions ask about a company's human resource policies and infrastructure that accompanies more established businesses.

Finally, the B Lab fee is based on total revenues of the

company it evaluates. As you become larger and more successful, your annual fee increases. Companies with a smaller top line pay less.

We encourage all companies to check out B Corp certification and start the B Lab assessment. It is an invaluable learning tool and provides the road map for reaching the highest level of standards as a Benefit Corporation. You'll find the evaluation tool educational and helpful to learn what is needed to be considered one of the top companies leading the movement toward sustainability, workforce empowerment and healthy communities by serving others. "The biggest change we've had since earning B Corp status is that we have become better at communicating," adds Amy Prosenjak of A To Z Wineworks. "Because B Lab makes you prove it."

Differences between a Benefit Corporation and a Certified B Corp:

Issues	Benefit Corporations	Certified B Corporations
Accountability	Directors/Members (LLCs) required to consider impact on all stakeholders	Same
Transparency	Must publish public report of overall social and environmental performance assessed against a third party standard*	Same
Performance	Self-reported	Must achieve minimum verified score on B Impact Assessment Recertification required every two years against evolving standard
Availability	Available for corporations only in 31 U.S. states and D.C.** and to LLCs in the states of Oregon and Maryland	Available to every business regardless of corporate structure, state, or country of incorporation
Cost	State filing fees from $70-$200	B Lab certification fees from $500 to $50,000/year, based on revenues

(According to Benefit Corp.net)
* Delaware benefit corps are not required to report publicly or against a third party standard
** Oregon and Maryland offer benefit LLC options

In our interviews (which you'll find transcripts of in the back of this book), a number of enlightened leaders offered comments about the differences. For example, "the B Lab certification process takes a lot of time, money and effort...although B Lab certification does carry with it well-respected brand recognition."

One other important fact to remember: you can easily convert to a Benefit Corporation even if you already incorporated with an existing operating license. Existing companies can elect to become a Benefit Corporation by amending their governing documents. There generally is a small fee (in some states it is free) for converting, but you can do it any time during the development and evolution of your business. And as previously mentioned, only in Oregon and Maryland, can LLCs become a Benefit Corporation.

If you are going to convert, you may want to obtain legal counsel before proceeding. Each state features slightly different regulations that need to be considered. Some are more complex than others and some states actually define and provide guidance around the type of public benefit that a Benefit Corporation can support.

For example, in Delaware, the legislation calls out the type of organizations a Benefit Corporation can support. These include a wide array of options such as:

- *Nutrition*: The delivery of nourishing, organic food to the nation's little ones and raising awareness and advancing solutions for childhood hunger and malnutrition in the United States.

- *Unemployment*: Build healthy communities, create jobs, and combat the social and economic ill effects of chronic joblessness in communities across America.

- *Education*: The Corporation also has a specific public benefit purpose to promote innovation in education and improved access to quality schooling.

- *Developing Countries*: Benefit international community development in developing countries.

- *Environmental Sustainability*: Increasing environmental sustainability by fostering and facilitating the reuse of durable goods.

Chapter 7
WHAT'S THE REAL VALUE OF BENEFIT CORPORATIONS

"We knew there were a lot of things missing from our organization to become 'best in class.' But once we understood, it was like finding your passion in education. We just went full throttle."

— Christian Ettinger, Brewmaster & Owner, Hopworks Urban Brewery

We found one of the best sources of general Benefit Corporation information to be benefitcorp.net. If you're looking for 7 compelling reasons to become a Benefit Corporation, here is what that website details. And yes, we do agree with all of them.

- *Reduced Director Liability*: Benefit Corporation status provides legal protection to balance financial and <u>non-financial</u> interests when making decisions.

- *Expanded Stockholder Rights*: Investing in a Benefit Corporation gives impact investors the assurance they need that they will be able to hold a company accountable to its mission in the future. This may attract investment capital.

- *A Reputation for Leadership*: Your business will join other high profile, highly-respected companies as a Benefit Corporation and be at the forefront of a growing movement.

- *An Advantage in Attracting Talent*: Millennials will grow to 75% of the workforce by 2025 and 77% of this demographic say their "company's purpose was part of the reason they chose to work there." Benefit Corporation status gives prospective employees confidence that a company is legally committed to their mission. (Data: Deloitte Millennial Survey)

- *Increased Access to Private Investment Capital:* Benefit Corporation status can make your company more attractive to investors as a company with increased legal protection, accountability and transparency around its mission. Benefit Corporations can also speed up investor due diligence since they produce an annual benefit report, which describes their qualitative activities aimed at producing general public benefit.

- *Increased Attractiveness to Retail Investors and Mission Protection as a Publicly Traded Company:* Benefit Corporations create an attractive investment opportunity for the same conscious consumers that have fueled organics, fair trade, and "buy local" movements, while enjoying a form of inoculation from the "short-termism" that plagues public equity markets.

- *Demonstration Effect:* Benefit Corporations show investors and entrepreneurs from every industry what the future Fortune 500 can look and act like.

We are not the only ones who feel the timing is right for this movement. "This is a long-term play," says Diane Henkels, Founder & Principal of Henkels Law. "And to be honest, it is hard to make this philosophy real in an economic sense. But this is what businesses need to do moving forward."

Chapter 8
ARE YOU READY TO TAKE THE PLUNGE?

"Becoming a B Corp helps you define the message of what you stand for. It is holistic. No other certification summarizes the standard we want to achieve."

— Augusto Carneiro, Founder & Chief Friendship Officer, Nossa Familia Coffee

Are you intrigued about the potential of becoming a Benefit Corporation? Maybe your business already practices some of the principles of the 3 P's. But is it right for you? Well to find out, we created a series of questions to help you make that decision to become a Benefit Corporation.

1. Does your management team regularly talk about how they can serve the community?

2. Do you hear employees and leaders frequently talk about recycling, biking, carpooling, and other "green" stuff?

3. Do you have compelling vision statement, or better yet a manifesto statement, that is emotional and gets employees excited about your company's purpose?

4. Do you pride yourself in giving employees a few extra perks to show you value them?

5. Do you have a fairly diverse workforce?

6. Do you want to help create healthy communities for ALL?

7. Are you thinking about workforce values like authenticity, simplicity, humility, sustainability and equity?

8. Does your team collaborate regularly or do you have more individual "rock stars?"

9. Do you have a large number of Millennials working

for your company?

10. Does your brand need a more emotional and uplifting message?

11. Do you have a policy that supports employees volunteering a certain number of hours a year?

12. Do you want to make a difference?

The more questions you answered "yes" to, the closer you are to the values of a Benefit Corporation. It is more about aligning your values and your employees' values with purpose. "I was disenchanted with the traditional business model and wanted to create a work environment to do good in the world," says Jaime Athos, CEO of Tofurky based in Hood River, Oregon. "I wanted to grow a company that's not about me, but the team."

Isn't that why we want to get up every morning? To feel we belong to something bigger than ourselves? We believe it's all summed up in the last question on our list: *Do you want to make a difference?*

Chapter 9
WHY THERE IS NO TURNING BACK

"People are waking up, driven by a personal purpose, wondering how they can run a business and give back to the greater community."

— *Hussein Al'Baity, CEO & Founder, The Printory*

We believe the time is now to join the movement to reinvigorate American businesses with honesty, transparency, and an appreciation for the "greater good." As you've learned in our book, Benefit Corporations and B Corps challenge the dated American business model of the individual hero and celebrate that we are all in this together.

The old paradigm of profit above all else and hero

worship of super-rich CEOs is succumbing to a humbler approach that values collaboration. It's the only way to save the planet from environmental toxicity. It's the only way to address the socio-economic disparities and inequities across the U.S.

You've seen the data from Nielsen, Deloitte, Cone and other respected research firms. Millennials and enlightened Boomers, along with members of more diverse communities, believe in these powerful principles and practices where the greater good for humanity is always front and center. And by whole-heartedly embracing such a powerful philosophy as the 3 P's, these savvy consumers with pocketbooks in hand will show their support for companies who demonstrate a commitment to social and environmental causes.

Through the process of researching, interviewing and writing our book, the two of us have become raving fans of the companies and leaders featured here as well as all Benefit Corporations, Benefit Companies, and B Corps across the country. As we currently witness all that is going on in the world, we're firmly convinced that there is no turning back. The practice of putting People and Planet first will mean more Profit for those who see the wisdom in it. Those who don't will suffer the consequences. It's really that simple.

We want to thank you for sharing your time with us. If our thinking resonates with you, we ask you to share this book and its ideas with friends and family. You see, we are at a crossroad in history. And it's our belief that the Benefit Corporation provides the path forward by putting soul into business.

Come join us in the revolution.

"If not us, who? If not now, when?"
— John F. Kennedy

INTERVIEW TRANSCRIPTS

Shannon Keith, CEO & Founder, Sudara, Inc.

Sudara Inc is a Benefit Company (Oregon's 'Benefit Corporation') committed to the creation of living wage jobs and opportunities for women in India who are the highest risk, or survivors of sex trafficking, and is dedicated to being a model for practicing, promoting and engaging business in socially responsible practices. https://www.sudara.org

"It's about making a real and significant impact on the community and on women's lives. We aren't here to get rich."

Why did you become a Benefit Company?
"We started out as a nonprofit but we wanted to have a greater and deeper impact and grow as a company. When Oregon passed the legislation allowing for incorporating as a Benefit Company, it was the right time to launch Sudara as a business."

What is appealing about being a Benefit Company?

"It aligns with our values as a company that does good and makes a significant impact. Creating jobs for individuals who have experienced the trauma of sex trafficking, employing them in the clothing industry and using the revenues to support them fulfills our mission. It's not about giving back, but rather it's about impact...really changing lives.

There is no downside to being a Benefit Company. I wonder why all businesses don't choose this model. I can't see a scenario where this structure would not be appropriate. We all want to build healthy communities."

What have you changed since becoming a Benefit Company?

"We hire for values incorporated in this model. It's not lip service or rhetoric. And employees that thrive here are individuals who share the same personal values as our company values."

What are the most important traits leaders of Benefit Companies bring to their organization?

"It's about transparency, integrity and being ethical. For the public good means doing the right thing even if it hurts! It is not personal gain, which can be a slippery slope if you only measure for profit. The business journey based on honesty is as important as monetary success. In addition, it is critical to believe and practice collaboration every day."

Augusto Carneiro, Founder & Chief Friendship Officer, Nossa Familia Coffee

Nossa Familia Coffee is a Portland, Oregon-based roaster whose passion is for roasting outstanding coffee sourced through deeply-rooted relationships. With family ties to over a century of coffee farming in the highlands of Brazil, today their direct trade tradition includes smallholder farms and cooperatives all over the world.
http://www.nossacoffee.com/

"We were donating to good causes to do good but we also were looking for a way to talk about it. The B Corp concept summarized what we wanted to do. We were inspired by New Seasons Market locally as well as Patagonia and Ben & Jerry's nationally."

How has the B Corp designation helped your business?
"Early on in the business, I felt a bit uncomfortable talking a lot about our good deeds. But slowly that changed. After all, we were making a positive impact on the planet. Why not share that with the world. We

marketed our products through New Seasons Market. The B Corp status strengthened our relationship. Once we officially became a B Corp, it almost immediately helped us win over new customers."

What's the most important trait for a B Corp leader?
"The most important trait is compassion. Empathy is a must. It's hard to be accountable when you're not empathetic."

What is the most important lesson you have learned in becoming a B Corp?
"I learned that customers want meaningful products to purchase. For example, last year we did a special holiday blend with some of the profits supporting a Nicaraguan farmer. The consumer thinks, 'I can purchase this and do something good, too.' Another important lesson for me is that we as a B Corp are helping shift the paradigm of what we think businesses should be."

Is being a B Corp part of the Nossa Familia brand message?
"It is most definitely a part of our brand message. It will soon be a part of all our packaging, and we also use

it in regard to our partnerships. For example, we collaborated on a cider with Hopworks, and are working on a wine partnership with A to Z Wineworks, which are both B Corps. Plain and simple, being a B Corp tells people you care not just about the bottom line, but the triple bottom line: people, planet, profit."

What is the single reason why you would suggest small businesses follow the model of Benefit Corporations and conscientious leadership?
"Becoming a B Corp helps you define the message of what you stand for. B Corp is holistic. No other certification summarizes the standard we want to achieve."

Hussein Al'Baity, CEO & Founder, The Printory

The Printory provides high quality, uniquely designed screen printing for T-shirts and other apparel including several projects for NIKE.
http://www.theprintory.com

"People are waking up, driven by a personal purpose, wondering how they can run a business and give back to the greater community. That's why I created the Refutee program, as an offshoot of my printing business. As my company grows and becomes more successful, we are committed to filling a container of t-shirts and distributing them free to refugees."

How has the Refutee Program helped your business?
"First, the program comes from our hearts. We are sincere and customers know that about us. They want to purchase printing from an organization that is compassionate and authentic."

What do your customers say?
"They tell us, we want to bring our business to a company that isn't driven solely by profit, rather that profit is the result of doing the business the right way

with staff that feels energized, supported and believes in giving back. I'm always surprised when they say the really respect me, when all I'm doing is sharing my bounty with others."

What have you learned as you practice this business model?

"First I realized that as CEO, I am the one who creates the vision of the future that is inclusive and generous. And I learned quickly that customers want to be a part of this. The Refutee program is a part of my branding and I have received a very positive response from customers."

What are the important traits of a Conscientious Leader?

"I've been inspired by TOMS shoes and other international cause-driven companies. What I have observed is that these businesses are compassionate, kind, authentic, inclusive in hiring, risk-takers and brave! These traits foster innovation and success. Those are the attributes of leadership I seek to bring to my team."

***What is the single reason why you would suggest
small businesses follow the model of Benefit
Corporations?***
"I'd tell them that people will notice and talk about you.
It creates a buzz when you have a value proposition
that is more than just about creating a product for sale
and profit. For us at The Printory, it is the only way to
grow our business, and every year since we started, our
sales have increased."

David Simnick, CEO, Soapbox

Soapbox is a manufacturer and distributor of personal care products throughout the world. 'Soap = Hope' as the company donates a bar of soap to developing communities with each bar purchased, while employing and purchasing local. http://www.soapboxsoaps.com

"From our humble beginnings, we wanted to create a company that was sustainable, a financial and operational engine that would support our mission to change the world and give children and families a chance."

Have you seen a change in culture since becoming a B Corp?
"It was always in our DNA, serving others, and the B Corp model reinforced who we are. It gave validity to our mission and supported our culture. At the end of the day, we wanted to create amazing products that provided a mechanism for giving back."

What was the process like in becoming a B Corp?
"It took us about 3 months and we had no idea where the journey would take us. But we approached it seriously and incorporated the principles and

approaches to running a business that were of the B Corp model. And one of the best things about becoming a B Corp is the community it creates, sharing best practices with like-minded leaders."

What are the most important traits of B Corp leaders?

"We are humble, yet remain hungry to make a success so we can fulfill our mission. I was a Boy Scout and we follow the Boy Scout slogan, 'do our duty to help other people at all times.' And at the end of the day, like many B Corps, we bring a sense of responsibility for the greater good. We are a bridge between nonprofits and the corporate world. We are business people that have an amazing product and a cause brand. It works for us."

Sarah Joannides, Director of Social Responsibility, New Seasons Market

New Seasons Market focuses on building and nourishing the communities they serve by creating lasting relationships with their customers, staff and vendors. https://www.newseasonsmarket.com

"The B Corp status helped us codify what we believed in. We knew what 'good' felt like. We knew about diverting waste and conservation efforts. But we weren't measuring results. 'Raising the bar' is part of being a B Corp. Four years later, we have a more embedded structure. We're more sure of our focus."

Can you give a specific example of how B Corp thinking has helped New Seasons Market?

"Doing the right thing is part of our values, but asking 'what is the impact of my bottom line' is more typical of business in general. We used that criteria in 2015 with the minimum wage issue in Oregon and asked ourselves, 'what is the right thing to do?' We weren't acting fast enough. Traditional business thinking is 'what can we afford?' We asked what feels right? How do we make our business model work for all stakeholders, not just shareholders."

Does being a B Corp help you attract employees?
"Millennials hear about our B Corp status. And it does attract talent out of school. People love B Corps and that's a reason why they come to us."

What is a significant lesson you as leader have learned in regard to B Corp?
"An important lesson we've learned is that being a B Corp leads to continual improvement and goal-setting. It helps direct activity and focus."

What is the single reason why you would suggest small businesses follow the model of Benefit Corporations and conscientious leadership?
"I would tell another business the single best reason to become a B Corp is your people. It is a valuable engagement tool. Millennials want to be a part of something 'bigger.' Being a B Corp is transparent. And we are doing work with authenticity."

Christian Ettinger, Brewmaster & Owner, Hopworks Urban Brewery

Hopworks Urban Brewery (HUB) is Portland's largest family-owned and operated brewery. HUB sources local ingredients to enrich the local economy and reduce their carbon footprint. http://hopworksbeer.com/

"We didn't know the full value until we got into. The reality came with the introspection while filling out the application. We knew there were a lot of things missing from our organization to become "best in class." But once we understood, it was like finding your passion in education. We just went full throttle."

Can you talk about the social significance for HUB in becoming a B Corp?

"It's kind of like earning the USDA stamp of approval. This is very much a long-term plan for us. I think it will be a decade before the real significance comes (to the general public). We asked ourselves, 'why not start with the deepest and most meaningful assessment of the Triple Bottom Line?' "

What positive outcome has your company experienced since becoming a B Corp?

"We are now more focused on pursuing the social 'people' leg of the Triple Bottom Line. Examples can be seen through our employee training, our approach to volunteerism, our approach to the workday as we offer more flexible conditions such as work from home, and our Bike To Work challenge. "

Would you recommend this model to your friends and competitors?

"Absolutely I would recommend this model to others. Businesses that don't have a way to quantify their sustainability claims is actually just their marketing department at work. Pursuing the Triple Bottom Line is reflection of a modern business reality. Everyone else will soon be playing catch-up."

What is the most important lesson you've learned through this process?

"It can be easy to lose sight of what matters to a company. Through B Corp, we have created a dashboard where we can measure objectives and chase success. We created an initiative for employees where social and environmental standards are measured."

Amy Prosenjak, President & COO, A To Z Wineworks

A to Z Wineworks is committed to making outstanding wines. It is matched by a belief in fair value and sustainability in business as well as farming and a drive to offer the highest quality for the best value. https://www.atozwineworks.com/

"We have always been a family-owned business. We had good intentions from the get go as we already initiated sustainable practices in the vineyard and winery prior to becoming a B Corp. What we liked about B Corp is that we had a third party telling us we were a sustainable business."

What's been the biggest change since becoming a B Corp?

"The biggest change we've had since earning B Corp status is that we have become better at communicating. Because B Lab makes you prove it. We supported volunteerism before, but we did not have proper HR documentation. We now promote it and offer 16 hours of volunteer time to each employee. The transparency made us a better company and enhanced our culture."

What is the most important trait to being a "Conscientious Leader?"

"Always be authentic. Present yourself with authenticity. Authenticity develops trust. Your true beliefs will always come through. You want to keep learning, keep assessing."

Is there an important lesson you've learned since becoming a B Corp?

"An important lesson we've learned from becoming a B Corp can be summed up in the B Corp motto, 'Measure what matters.' You can't improve things if you can't measure. It's important to understand what you're measuring. It's as applicable to business life as it is to personal life."

What is the single best reason you'd give another company to become a B Corp?

"Single biggest reason to become a B Corp is that it drives all three bottom lines. The certification gives you credit for all three: environment, social and economic. Our B Corp status resonates across all age demographics. There simply is a very strong interest in the model."

Jon Blumenauer, CEO, The Joinery

The Joinery creates handcrafted furniture that is here for good, a nod to the lifetime warranty on all its residential furniture, as well as the company's significant investment in its employees, environmental performance, and the broader community. https://www.thejoinery.com/

"I think that we as a society are increasingly looking to create meaning in our lives, and one of the ways that happens is that people make purchasing decisions based on alignment with their core values. So in that context, being a B Corp is helpful because it quickly makes a statement about your values, and establishes credibility that your business makes significant investment that benefits society as a whole."

What challenges are there in becoming a B Corp?
"It's a lot of work to become a B Corp. The certification process is rigorous, and requires a lot of time as well as access to information about how your business is run, and the documentation to back that up. It is also challenging to communicate what it means to your team and other key stakeholders."

What is the most important trait to being a "Conscientious Leader?"

"I believe the most important trait for a leader in this space is commitment, demonstrated on a variety of levels. Commitment to your purpose. To getting better. To accepting accountability. To the team. Humility is also critical – although we have accomplished some good things, we all have a lot of room to learn, grow and improve. Recognizing that is the first step to making it happen."

Have you experienced any positive outcomes since becoming a B Corp?

"A great benefit to our B Corp status has been in attracting new talent. Over the past year we have had a number of interview candidates come to us because we were a B Corp and they wanted to work for a company that shared their values. This has helped us bring some great new people on board, who are providing energy and leadership to improve further. And although not very sexy, we have also had significant success with improved resource usage, lowering our use of electricity by 20%, water by 40% and natural gas by 12% over in the past three years."

***What is the single best reason you'd give another
company to become a B Corp?***
"Best reason I'd tell a business friend or colleague to
become a B Corp is that it builds resiliency in your
business. Adopting this business model offers meaning
to people, to all stakeholders. And the framework is
there to identify ways to strengthen your organization."

Jaime Athos, CEO, Tofurky

Tofurky manufactures and distributes nationally, a vegetarian turkey replacement using a blend of organic tofu and wheat protein.
http://tofurky.com/

"The B Corp spirit is alive and well in our company. Social purpose values are personal to me, as I was disenchanted with the traditional business model and wanted to create a work environment to do good in the world. Growing a company that's not about me but the team. Tofurky is about more than a paycheck; it about our employees; it's about the pride in contributing to a better world - delivering value while earning money."

How has being a B Corp impacted employees?
"I believe it provides meaning to our staff as they see that their contributions aren't about earning more money, but about learning and doing things better in a way that serves both our customers and our employees. Our brand and products are a platform for 'other-oriented' people who actualize and reflect values that support our community, people, animals and nature."

Does being a B Corp help you attract employees?
"We believe in work-life balance, and our benefits
reflect this, which helps in recruitment. People who
join our workforce also like that our culture is about
the collective and not the celebrity worker -- that
together they can make a difference. This is appealing
when they come to us. And they like our 'Volunteerism
Program,' where we can compensate employees when
they volunteer with the community. We encourage our
staff to participate in volunteer activities that interest
them. We are helping the wind along the way blowing
in the direction of healthier communities."

*What is the most important trait of a B Corp
leader?*
"It's about being values driven and having a
commitment to the community, practicing authenticity,
and transparency with your employees and setting an
example for corporate peers."

*What is a significant lesson you as a leader have
learned in regard to B Corps?*
"You commit to the B Corp values with a recognition
that you reap the benefits long-term. It is building a

reputation that will pay you back, a win-win scenario, although it may not be immediate."

What is the single reason why you would suggest small businesses follow the model of Benefit Corporations and B Corps?
"More and more consumers resonate with the principles of B Corps. They look for authenticity and value companies that are dedicated to helping one another out, to contributing to the community, and something I learned as a child growing up in a small town."

Mac Prichard, Founder & President, Prichard Communications

Prichard Communications provides strategic communications, marketing and public relations to changemakers across the U.S. including the Robert Wood Johnson Foundation. http://www.prichardcommunications.com/

"Being a B Corp is such a great fit as it reflects our fundamental values, providing clients with communications to make a better world."

What is special about being a B Corp?
"B Corps represent small but influential companies committed to being leaders in changing communities for the better -- we are kindred spirits."

What benefits has your company reaped from being a B Corp?
"It's a powerful recruiting tool, particularly with Millennials. This model really appeals to people who want to work not just for money but to make a difference. Also, our clients like it and it has helped us

win quite a few RFPs. It's a competitive edge for us. Our vendors like it, too. We believe putting people front and center helps us prosper. Finally, becoming a B Corp encouraged us to look at all our business practices to ensure alignment with B Corp standards and that make us much more thoughtful about policies and procedures, including benefits."

What have you changed since becoming a B Corp?
"We put a lot more energy and effort into supporting our employees and using more sustainable practices. We now offer our staff annual bus passes, we compost regularly, and our financials are much more transparent."

What are the most important traits B Corp leaders bring to their companies?
"It's important to be a good listener, open to learning from customers, staff and partners. Humility is critical and always emphasize service to others. I've learned the more I give, the more I get."

Diane Henkels, Founder & Principal, Henkels Law

Henkels Law provides legal support advocating, informing and empowering on behalf of clients in Indian and tribal, energy and utility, and small business contracting. http://www.henkelslaw.com

"Being a Benefit Company supports a corporate shift in approach that is growing today. It is not philanthropic but rather communicates a way of doing business where people, planet and profit equals purpose and transparency around how that is done. This thinking is not going to be obsolete."

How has being a Benefit Company enhanced your practice?

"I think that it has more to do with other things like marketing and packaging the message versus economic benefits. It does simplify how I describe my practice. I don't need to use a lot of words to explain what I do and my approach. I just state I am a Benefit Company and people can look that up and understand the foundation of the firm. It's a quick way to get the message out around what I believe. This designation may have also helped me with procurement."

Has the culture changed at your firm since designation?

"I was one of the early adopters in Oregon and provided legal counsel to some companies among the inaugural group of Oregon businesses that became the first Benefit Companies. So it is something I have believed in and embraced from the beginning. Subsequently, as I work with colleagues and contractors, everyone knows up front and is aware and sometimes aligned with this philosophy and culture."

Any lessons learned over the past few years as a Benefit Company?

"This is a long-term play. And to be honest, it is hard to make this philosophy real, in an economic sense. But this is what businesses need to do moving forward. So it is aspirational for me, as I still have to focus on profit and loss and business strategy. But long-term, I believe this is the right way to go."

***What are the most important traits to have as a
conscientious leader?***
"Don't rule things out. Be open to opportunities to
partner and create synergy. My grandparents were
entrepreneurs during the Depression. Yet with their
employees, they always were fair and supported them
ala Benefit Company values. They were leaders!"

RESOURCES

Books

Friedman, Milton, <u>Capitalism and Freedom</u>, University of Chicago Press, 1962.

Mackey, John and Sisodia, Raj, <u>Conscious Capitalism – Liberating the Heroic Spirit of Business,</u> Harvard Business School Publishing Corporation, 2012.

Ray, Paul and Booth, Sherry, <u>Cultural Creatives: How 50 Million People are Changing the World,</u> Crowne/Archetype, 2001.

Internet Citations

B Lab, "What are B Corps?" https://www.bcorporation.net/what-are-b-corps, 2017.

Benefitcorp.net, "Why Is a Benefit Corporation Right

for Me?" http://benefitcorp.net/businesses/why-become-benefit-corp, 2017.

Bradbury, Mark, Huffington Post, "The 7 Incredible Facts About Boomer Spending" http://www.huffingtonpost.com/mark-bradbury/the-7incredible-facts-about-boomers-spending, May 17, 2015.

Cone Communications, "Millennials CSR Study" http://www.conecomm.com/research-blog/2015-cone-communications-millennial-csr-study, 2015.

Khahili, Olivia, "Conscious Capitalism, A Method for Prosperity" http://causecapitalism.com/conscious-capitalism-a-mechanism-for-prosperity/, April 2011.

Deloitte Millennial Survey, "Big Demands, High Expectations", https://www2.deloitte.com/content/dam/Deloitte/global/Documents/About-Deloitte/gx-dttl-2014-millennial-survey-report.pdf, January 2014

Edelman, "Good Purpose Study" http://www.edelman.com/insights/intellectual-property/good-purpose/, 2012.

Forbes Magazine, "Conscious Capitalism" https://www.forbes.com/sites/fredsmith/2016/11/11 /lessons-from-a-decade-of-conscious-capitalism/#549fb48a2e0c, Nov. 11, 2016.

Hermes, Jennifer, "Baby Boomers Believe in Sustainable Principles and Will Pay for Them" https://www.environmentalleader.com/2012/02/stud y-baby-boomers-believe-in-sustainable-principles-and-will-pay-for-them/, Feb. 29, 2012.

Horowitz, Bruce, " Millennials Spur Capitalism with a Conscience" https://www.usatoday.com/story/money/business/20 13/03/25/kindness-panera-bread-nordstrom-starbucks/1965183/#, March 25, 2013.

Hower, Mike, "The Greenest Generation Ever, Boomers or Millennials?" http://www.triplepundit.com/2013/04/greenest-generation-baby-boomers-millennials/, April 25, 2013

Hunt, Vivian, McKinsey & Company, "Why Diversity

Matters", http://www.mckinsey.com/business-functions/organization/our-insights/why-diversity-matters , January 2015.

Khahili,Olivia, "Conscious Capitalism, A Method for Prosperity, http://causecapitalism.com/conscious-capitalism-a-mechanism-for-prosperity/, April 2011.

Nielsen Global Survey, "Doing Well by Doing Good" http://www.nielsen.com/us/en/insights/reports/2014/doing-well-by-doing-good.html, June 17, 2014.

Oregon Secretary of State Office, "How to Become a Benefit Company" http://sos.oregon.gov/business/Pages/benefit-company.aspx, 2016.

Schwartz, Tony, Harvard Business Review, "Companies that Practice Conscious Capitalism Perform 10x Better" https://hbr.org/2013/04/companies-that-practice-conscious-capitalism-perform, April 04, 2013.

Wazwaz, Noor, US News, "It's Official: The U.S. is Becoming a Minority-Majority Nation"

http://www.usnews.com/news/articles/2015/07/06/i
ts-official-the-us-is-becoming-a-minoritymajority-
nation, July 6, 2015

ABOUT the AUTHORS

Mary Anne Harmer is the co-author of the book *25 Building Blocks to Create a Conscientious Organization*. She is senior strategist and partner of HCollaborative, Conscientious Leadership and Communication, an Oregon Benefit Company. The blog for the firm features more than 100 posts on leadership and communication. She and her partner have put on numerous business workshops throughout the Northwest on strategic visioning, manifesto development and how to become a benefit corporation. Mary Anne is an active leader in social justice issues in the state of Oregon. She lives in Aloha, Oregon.

Tom Hering is the co-author of the book *25 Building Blocks to Create a Conscientious Organization*. He is creative director and partner of HCollaborative. He also wrote *51 Life Lessons Every Boomer Male Should Have Learned by*

Now and founded the lifestyle site boomermale.com, devoted to men of the baby boomer generation. He serves as advocacy co-chair for the Interfaith Alliance on Poverty, a group whose mission is to help alleviate poverty in the Portland metro area. He lives in Portland, Oregon.

The authors have launched BenefitCorporationsforGood.com, a resource for businesses seeking to become or are already established benefit corporations. The site will feature articles, tips and advice for companies believing in and practicing the 3 P's of People, Planet and Profit.

Made in the USA
Middletown, DE
11 January 2018